Art Editor Toni Rann
Senior Editor Jane Yorke
Photography Stephen Oliver
Series Consultant Neil Morris
Editorial Director Sue Unstead
Art Director Anne-Marie Bulat

This is a Dorling Kindersley Book
published by Random House, Inc.

First American edition, 1990

Library of Congress Cataloging-in-Publication Data
My first look at shapes.
p.   cm.
Summary: Photographs explore the concept of shapes,
including squares, circles, rectangles, and diamonds.
ISBN 0-679-80534-6
1. Geometry - Juvenile literature. [1. Shape.]
I. Random House (Firm)
QA445.5.M9 1990
516.2 - dc20 89-63087 CIP AC

Manufactured in Italy   2 3 4 5 6 7 8 9 0

Phototypeset by Windsorgraphics, Ringwood, Hampshire
Reproduced in Hong Kong by Bright Arts
Printed in Italy by L.E.G.O.

· MY · FIRST · LOOK · AT ·

Shapes

Random House 🏠 New York

Circles

yo-yo

softball

flower

clock

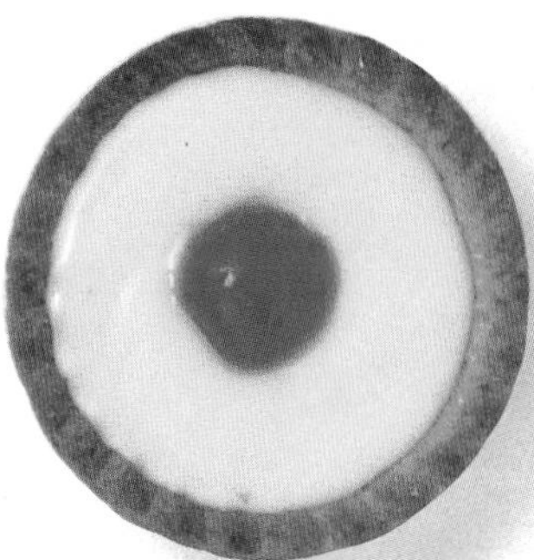

tart

beads

cookies

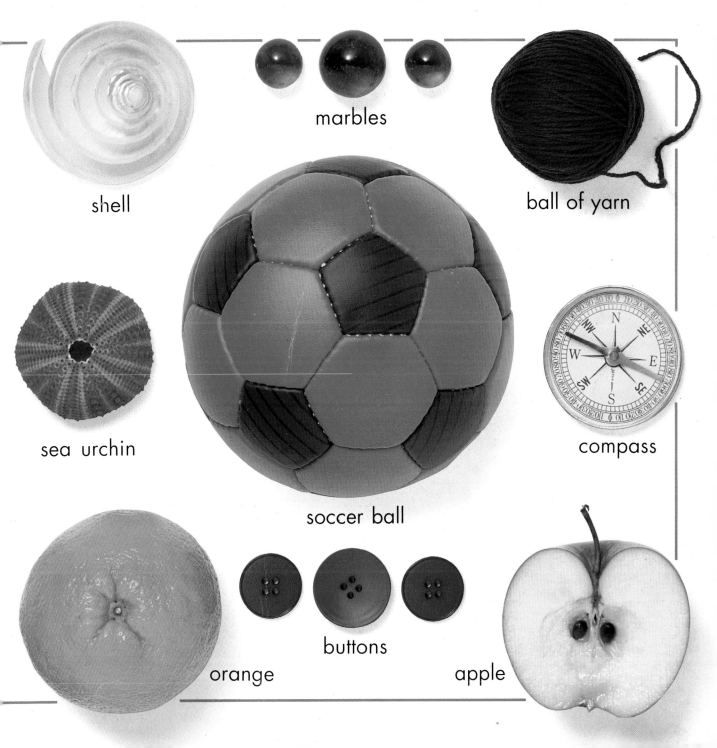

shell

marbles

ball of yarn

sea urchin

soccer ball

compass

orange

buttons

apple

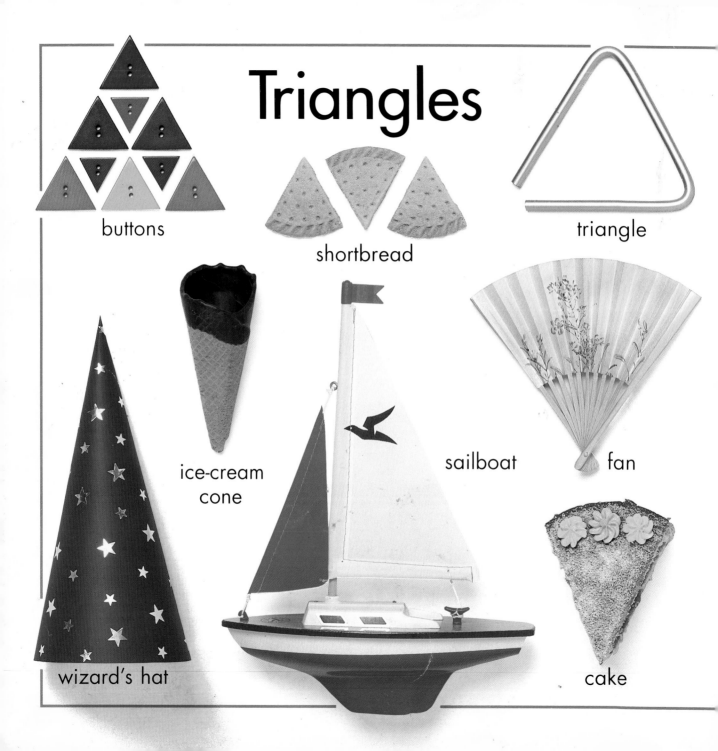

Triangles

buttons

shortbread

triangle

ice-cream cone

sailboat

fan

wizard's hat

cake

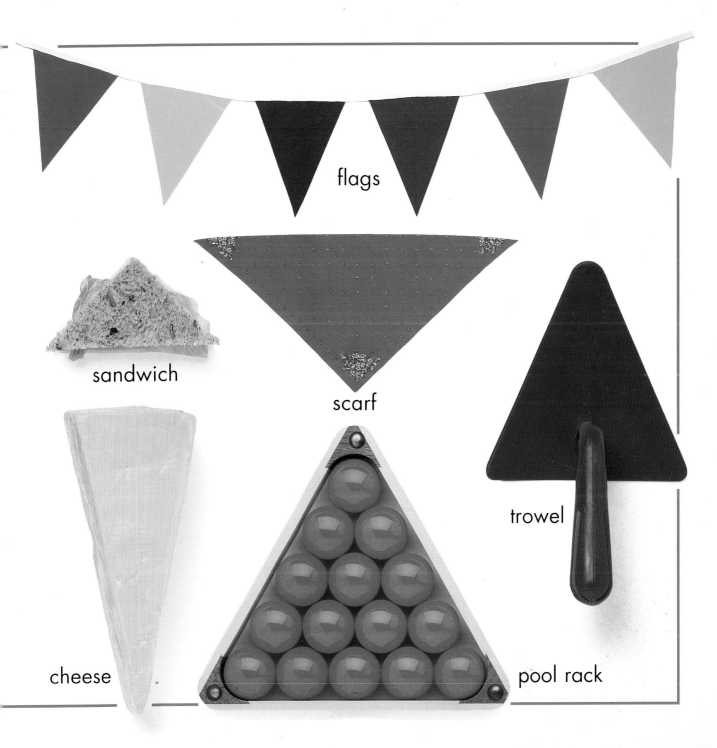

flags

sandwich

scarf

cheese

pool rack

trowel

Squares

cloth

candy

book

building blocks

present

box

tile

die

handkerchief

pincushion

clock

jack-in-the-box

baby blocks

Rectangles

bag

barrette

chocolate bar

eraser

shoe box

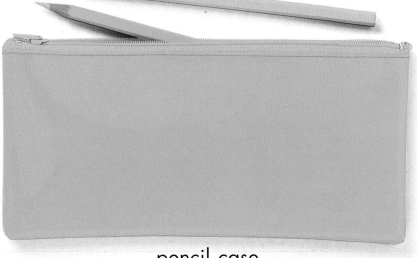
pencil case

paintbox

envelope

cookie

ruler

buckle

picture

door

brick

door

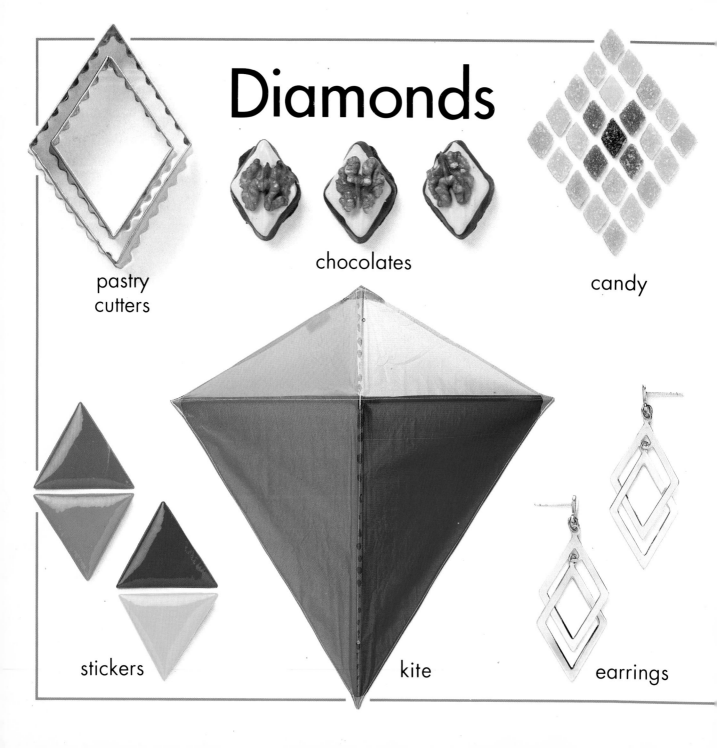

Diamonds

pastry
cutters

chocolates

candy

stickers

kite

earrings

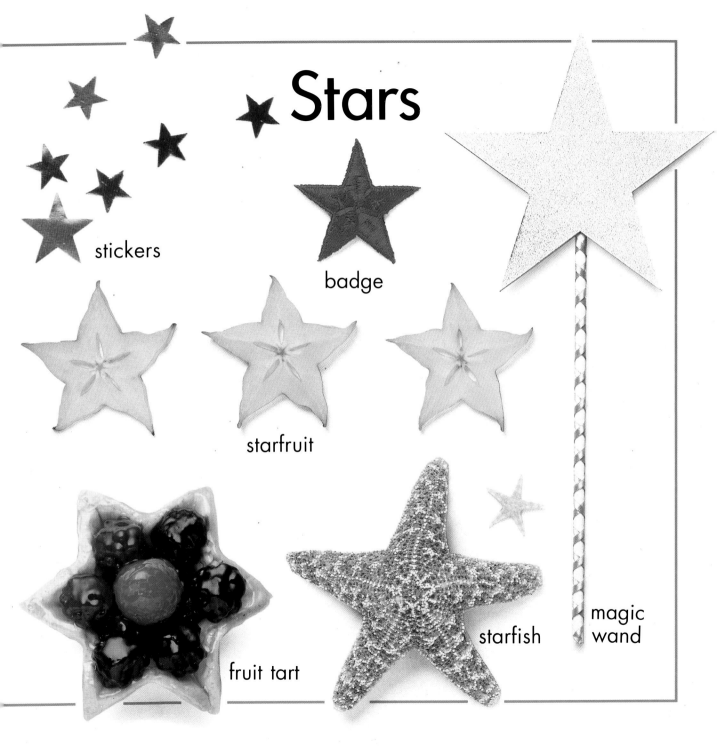

Stars

stickers

badge

starfruit

fruit tart

starfish

magic
wand

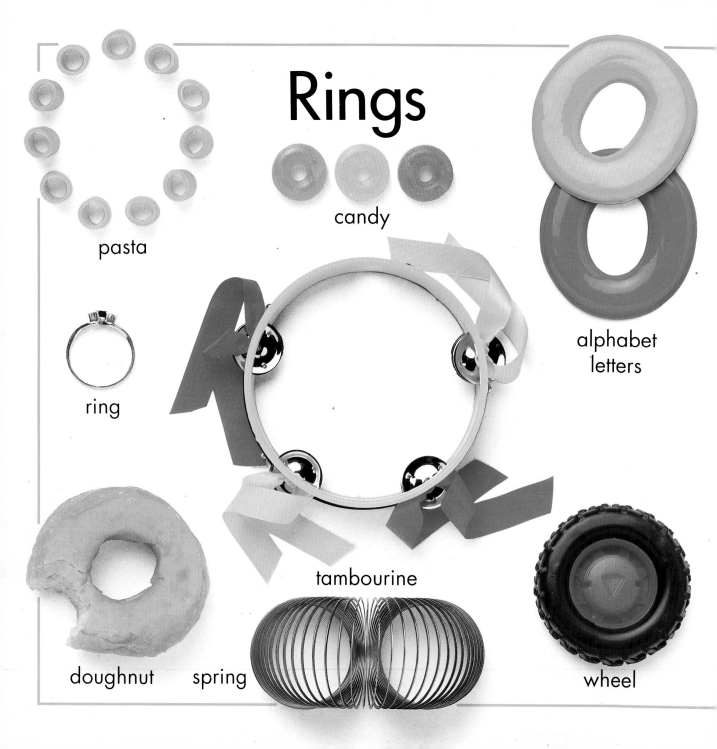

Rings

pasta

candy

alphabet
letters

ring

tambourine

doughnut   spring

wheel

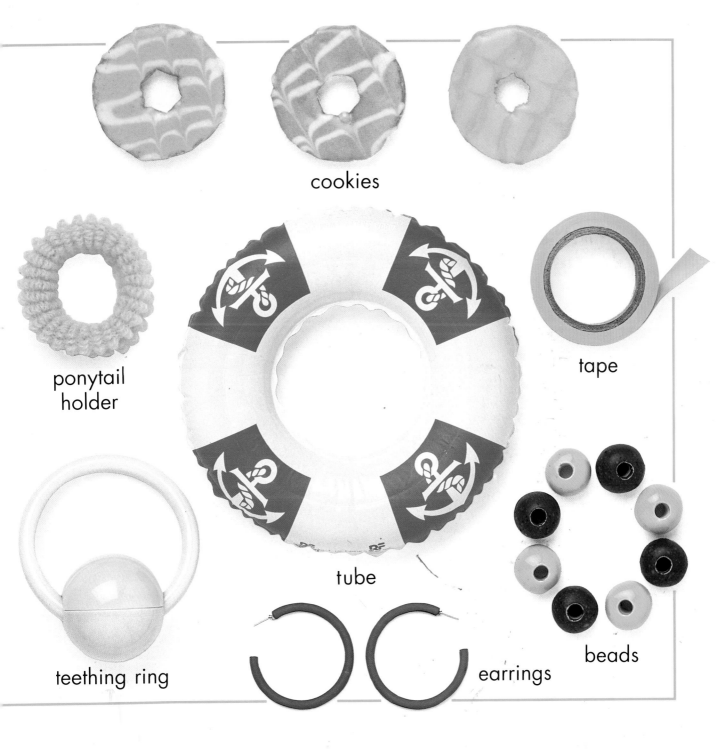

cookies

ponytail
holder

tape

teething ring

tube

earrings

beads

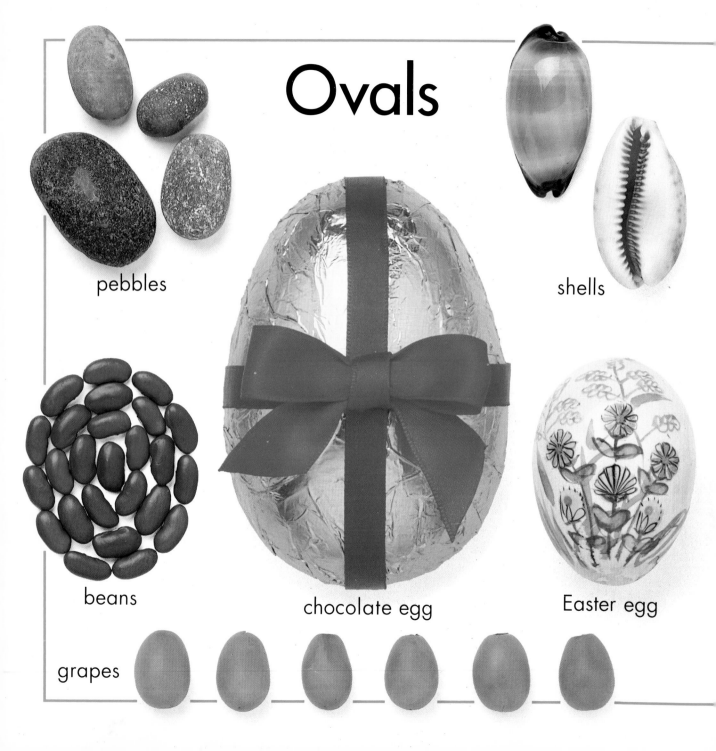

Ovals

pebbles

shells

beans

chocolate egg

Easter egg

grapes

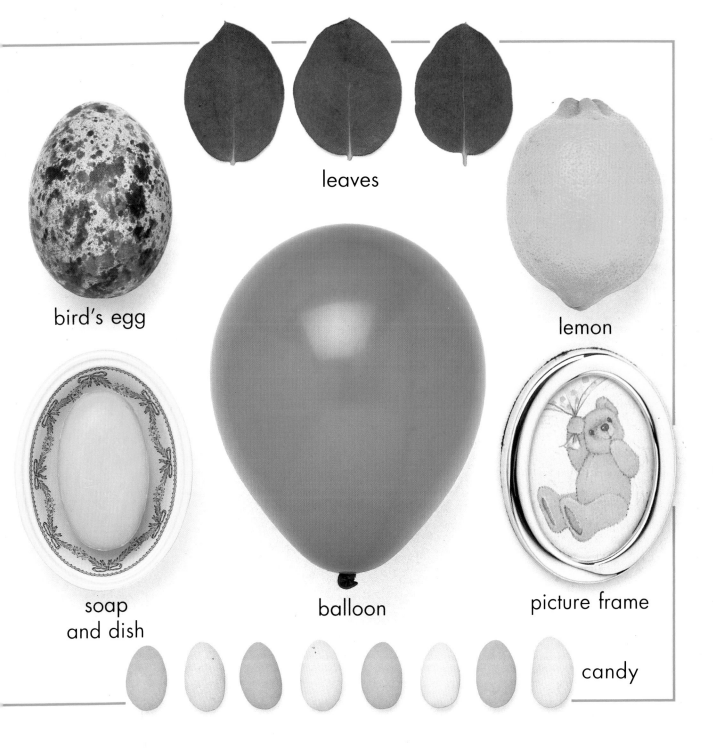

leaves

bird's egg

lemon

soap
and dish

balloon

picture frame

candy

Hearts

sequins

buttons

chocolate

pencil
sharpener

lollipops

ten of
hearts

sachet

pastry
cutters

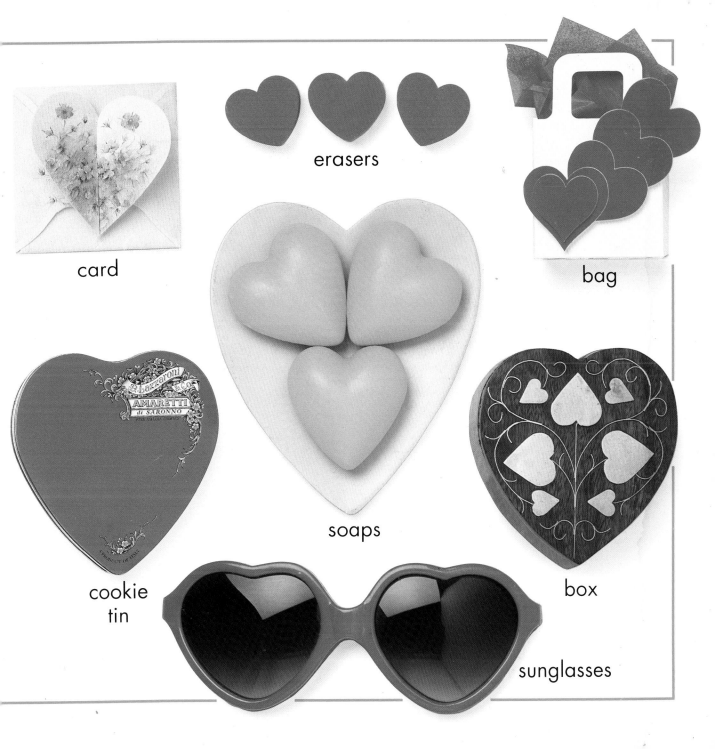

erasers

card

bag

soaps

cookie
tin

box

sunglasses